A Dying Language

Monica Corish

Foreword by Sharon Foley, CEO Irish Hospice Foundation

Acknowledgements

Thanks are due to the editors of the following journals, newspapers, anthologies and websites in which these poems, or versions of these poems, have appeared: *Poetry Ireland Review; The Stinging Fly; THE SHOp; Orbis; The North; The Interpreter's House; Crannóg Magazine;* [The Galway Review;](#) [Ink, Sweat and Tears;](#) *Seventh Quarry;* [North-West Words;](#) *Boyne Berries;* [The Irish Medical Journal;](#) *Causeway/Cabhsair; Artemis; Ariadne's Thread;* [The Bow Wow Shop;](#) *The Leitrim Observer; Africa Magazine; The 2014 Hippocrates Prize Anthology; The 2016 Hippocrates Prize Anthology;* and *Ten Years in the Doghouse.*

Thanks also to the judges of the following competitions: 'Back Where We Started' won the 2013 North West Words/Donegal Creameries Poetry Prize; 'Lady Rain' was shortlisted for the same prize in 2012; 'The Skill of Lipstick' and 'A Dying Language' were commended for the Hippocrates Prize for Poetry and Medicine in 2014 and 2016 respectively; and 'Stripped of Everything', 'A Dying Language' and 'The Doorway into the Invisible' were finalists in the 2015 Pat Schneider Poetry Competition.

I am very grateful to the Arts & Disability Awards Ireland scheme for a writing and mentoring bursary that allowed me to work closely with Gréagóir Ó Dúill, PhD. I owe a debt of deep gratitude to Gréagóir for his compassionate objectivity, rigourous critique, and skillful encouragement. Without him, these poems would be less than they are. My thanks also to Leitrim Arts Office for a writing bursary. I am grateful to the members of The Poets' Cauldron – Anne O'Connell, Eilo Molloy, Paula Lahiff, Dermot Lahiff and Carol Wilson – for their good questions and good humour; and to Annie Deppe, for her insightful comments on the penultimate draft of the manuscript.

I am grateful beyond telling to my sisters Mary and Breda, and to my brother Mike, for loving and struggling with me through the months of our mother's final illness, and through the time after her death when our father lived with my brother and his wife and daughters. Our extended family – sister-in-law, brothers-in-law, nieces and aunt – made it possible for my parents to die in their own beds. Our thanks to the people of Doon and environs – they were the "compassionate community" that every dying person needs; and to Milford Hospice Home Care Team and Meath Community Palliative Care Service – without their skilful aid, our parents could not have died at home. I am grateful also to Sharon Foley, Orla Keegan, and Angela Edghill of the Irish Hospice Foundation for their enthusiastic response to this collection.

And last, and first: thanks and love to Tom Sigafoos for his support – emotional, practical, and literary – and for his continuing presence in my life.

Copyright © 2016 Monica Corish
Foreword © 2016 Sharon Foley, CEO Irish Hospice Foundation

All rights reserved. No part of this publication may be reproduced or used in any manner whatsoever without the express written permission of the publisher except for the use of brief quotations in a book review or scholarly journal. Requests to publish extracts should be addressed in the first instance to Monica Corish www.monicacorish.ie.

Cover design: Tom Sigafoos
Cover image: Poppy at Sunset, Susanne Nilsson/Flickr goo.gl/0LXziW,
Creative Commons Attribution-ShareAlike 4.0 International License

First Printing: 2016
ISBN 978-0-9931534-4-0

Published by the Irish Hospice Foundation
Morrison Chambers (4th Floor)
32 Nassau Street
Dublin 2
D02 YE06
www.hospicefoundation.ie

50% of profits from the sale of this book will go to the Irish Hospice Foundation and to local Hospices.

Further copies are available through www.barnesandnoble.com, www.amazon.com and directly from the author at www.monicacorish.ie

This publication was supported by a 2013 grant from Arts and Disability Awards Ireland, funded by the Arts Council of Northern Ireland and the Arts Council / An Chomhairle Ealaíon, and managed by the Arts and Disability Forum; and by a 2013 bursary from Leitrim Arts Office.

In loving memory of Teresa Corish *née* Houlihan, 28/1/1932 – 1/11/2011,
and Michael Corish, 25/9/1923 – 25/7/2013

And for Hospice Home Care Nurses everywhere

Contents

Acknowledgements 3
Foreword 9
The North West Hospice Needs Your Help 11

By nightfall everything has changed

Garden, Twilight 15
Phone Call, Columbia River Gorge 16
Sewing Silk 17
Still Upright 18
Grace-of-the-Goddess 19
Fetish 20
Anubis 21
In the car driving home from the hospital 22
Someone puts a cup of tea in his hand 23

A storm that blows all maps away

Raiméis 27
Hitting the Rapids 29
Side-effects may occur, including euphoria 30
Show Time with Teresa 31
Thunder, No Rain 32
A Dying Language 33
Bargaining 34
Planets to Her Dying Sun 35
Time on the Ocean 36
Homing 37
The battles we fight when we can't win the war 38
Rough 39
Agitation, in Three Movements 40
Recompense 42
A Dream of Dark Wings 43
Dust 44
Wild Love 45

The dead are gathering to gather you in

Stripped of Everything.. 49
Mater... 50
Seven Winters 51
Respite 52
Give me the Death I Need... 53
The House of the Double-Headed Axe................................... 54
Rage... 55
Bitter Honey.. 56
Back Where We Started 57
Daughter Number Two 58
The Skill of Lipstick 59
Wing Mirror, Butterfly 60
The Doorway into the Invisible 61
Between *Samhain* and All the Saints...................................... 63
The Wake 64
Final Intimacies... 65

Tears come, a salt surprise

Filling the Skip 69
Advice from My Dead Mother 70
Fetish, Reprise... 71
Lady Rain... 72
The Butcher, The Lacemaker.. 73
My Father Faced Death in Full Knowledge 74
Imbolc... 75
Caprice.. 76
The Old World Slips Away... 77
Grief, Uncomplicated... 79
Dreamtime 80

Glossary.. 81
About the author 82

Foreword

Dying, death, loss and bereavement are enduring themes in poetry. Each of us hold special poems in our hearts and memories. We intrinsically understand the power of poetry to transform, to nourish and to comfort in time of loss and grief.

I remember so clearly those poems from my own school curriculum (who could forget Emily Dickinson… *Because I could not stop for Death, He kindly stopped for me; The carriage held but just ourselves, And Immortality*) but I stopped reading poetry after the infamous leaving certificate exams. However, I surprised myself by turning to poetry many times in adulthood – to help me understand the profound experience of new life, of death and of grief. Seamus Heaney, John O'Donohue, William Butler Yeats, Patrick Kavanagh and Khalil Gibran have all brought me comfort and solace at different times. For me, poetry touches my soul and helps me understand and remember - I am sure many share this experience.

It was a joy to sit and read Monica's beautiful work as she traces the emotion and experience of being with someone as they face dying. Hospice is about living well to the end and Monica's poems embody this spirit, but with cutting honesty - she does not hide from the struggle this living can involve. The dance of language, of knowing and not knowing that death is near, of sharing and hiding, of anger and tenderness, make Monica's poems worthy additions to the canon of grief poetry.

She describes in such eloquent ways grief and emotional rawness, relationships reconstructed, her "grief, uncomplicated":

We did well, mother of mine: I grew to love you
straight, without tangles of need;
you loved me honest, the way I always wanted.
Dying, you looked me in the eye.

We are delighted that Monica chose to highlight the Hospice cause in her work. She reminds us we will all need each other's help at some time. Hospice is a community initiative; each county has vibrant fundraising committees, activities and events that bring people together in the cause of others. By supporting Monica's work, you too are helping this great cause.

Monica's poems will spread across Ireland, a fitting tribute to the complex caring work carried out in each county for people who are at their most vulnerable and most in need. We wish Monica well in her work and I hope you enjoy the poems as much as I did.

Sharon Foley

CEO Irish Hospice Foundation, 2016

The North West Hospice Needs Your Help
Leitrim Observer Headline, July 18 2014

And you need theirs.
Though today you are
healthy, a trout
swimming through rainbows;
though your mother is
young as a girl at heart;
though your father is
sturdy, a great black ox;
all will change,
this play will end,
you will need their help.

By nightfall everything has changed

Garden, Twilight

Teresa
will you come in out of the garden,
you'll catch your death.
She doesn't hear him,
her hearing-aid switched off
as long as she can see her poppies,
the orientals still scarlet as pimpernels
in the slow exhalation of twilight.

Her bare hands dig down
into the umber, crumbling earth,
her beloved.
She cradles roots like babies,
transplants each treasure into the soil
best suited to its nature,
into sunshine, shade,
half-shade.

He calls again,
from the back door this time:
Bet love, will you not come in?
his pet name for her returning
with his need: *It's damp,*
you'll catch your death.

She doesn't answer.
The falling dark
finally drives her in.

Phone Call, Columbia River Gorge

After one false turn we find our way
onto Highway 30: Troutdale, Crown Vista,
Bridal Veil, Multnomah Falls. We come upon
a gallery of First Nations art: Wolf Teeth;
Eagle Eye; Thunderbird (a creature of myth
so powerful its wings make thunder
and trouble, lightning bolts out of its eyes);
Raven Wing; Salmon Scale; Hummingbird.

A text arrives on the mobile:
There is urgent news, but not immediate.
I'm not surprised.
My father lives on borrowed time.
I call my sister: *It's Dad?*
Her voice is trembling: *No. It's Mam.*
It seems to be lung cancer.
They say that she is dying.

I drift the gallery searching for sense.
Plate-glass windows face east, up river -
giant conifers, Sequoia and Redwood,
a wilderness of trees old as history.
This circle of Cedar is a Mandala,
all of creation, fire and wind, wave and star.
On a raw white wall a blue Orca, the curve
of her body doubled over, is eating a Seal.

I call my mother.
She won't let me talk about it,
didn't want me told till I got home,
wants to hear about our holiday.

Trouble is homeless. The Thunderbird
stirs storms in Ireland. The *Bean Sí* wails death
in the Pacific Northwest.

Sewing Silk

When the consultant says:
I'm booking you in for next Tuesday, the 17th,
for more tests, you ask for time*:*
Please can we make it the 18th?
There's a do in the golf club on Tuesday night.

You sound hoarse on the phone:
There's a little blood in my cough
from that tube down my throat, that camera thing,
but that dress I got in one of 'those' shops for only €20?
I found the perfect bolero to go with it,
the most gorgeous colour, a deep peach.
All I need now is to adjust it
in time for the dance. I'm so glad
I have something to do while I'm waiting.
I need to take it in, just a little bit.
Your father is setting the sewing machine for silk.

Still Upright

So dry
a sinkhole of earth has fallen

One conifer,
roots half in earth half in air

Like the crab
that tightens its grip on your windpipe

Still upright
until the next hard rainfall

Grace-of-the-Goddess
for Danielle and Heather Corish

I remember, from when I was old enough to remember,
the four of us getting ready for bed, slipping out of day-clothes
into pyjamas: We watch as she moves, half dressed,
between the bathroom and the bedroom, her white satin slip

beneath her dressing gown, her face changing, eyelashes lengthening,
eyebrows arcing, lips as red as Smarties; while our father fusses
with keys, phone numbers, instructions for the babysitter,
with telling us we should be in bed by now.

We plead: *Just five minutes more. Please?*
She appears out of the bedroom: her bare shoulders,
her leaf-green satin dress held up by the grace-of-god,
her night-time perfume, diamanté jewellery, a necklace with stones

as big as sixpences. She clips a pendant earring to her left ear,
to her right ear, turns to face us: *How do I look?*

Fetish

My mother believes that what can be held,
touched, smelled, is more than a reminder, is alive.
An object - button, book, creased letter -
is as a mask to a tribe in the Suud
or a carved ivory tusk to an Inuit.
It holds the imprint of its maker, of every owner,
the oils of their skin rubbed in. It shines
with presence, existence, essence.

She keeps buttons for possible future use and for memory:
this wafer-thin disc is an interior fastener
for the pink organza she wore only once,
to her brother's son's wedding;
this tiny mother-of-pearl is a wrist-button,
never sewn back, from the Alice-blue kid gloves
she wore to a dress-dance in her twenties,
three months pregnant with me.

Anubis
i.m. Patrick Houlihan

A small white dog
boards the train in Mullingar.

I'm travelling from Leitrim to Limerick
for the first time since I heard your news.

He jumps into the seat beside me,
I put him out of the seat to find his owner.

He claims no one, no one claims him.
He heads off

down the length of the carriage,
into the next carriage, on an adventure.

Off to Dublin, for a day of shopping?
To see the Frida Kahlo exhibition?

I wish he was beside me still,
warm beneath my hands.

A dog is good about the house
when death is in the air.

You remember? Your brother, Pat,
was dying, the air was thick with fear.

A neighbour brought a pup to visit,
a chocolate Labrador,

he licked death's face and hand, he offered
death the paw, he took the living for a walk.

This small white dog, this gift -
I should have brought him home to you.

In the car driving home from the hospital

the backseat overflows: your overnight case;
two carrier bags, your one-day stay expanded
into seven days and nights of waiting for tests
and answers; two outsize bags from the pharmacy
crammed with only comfort; a green snake
of healing on a blank white ground.

You ask me a question:
And do I have cancer?

    Yes.

But, you say, *of the hopeful,
manageable kind.*

I take my eyes off the traffic to look at you.
The consultant took me aside this morning
before she discharged you into my care,
showed me the scan of your lungs,
an x-ray of your right hip.
Her initial prognosis - two years -
has shrivelled to two months.
You catch my eye, look away.

No question.
I keep on driving.

Someone puts a cup of tea in his hand

i
She begs him to hire a carer
for the days when she is out all day:
playing golf, travelling to Knock
on the parish pilgrimage, to Cork
to visit her slowly dying sister.
For her peace of mind.

Though his lungs are ruined
with emphysema; his airways
narrowed and congested; though the orbit
of his life spirals closer each year
to the oxygen machine; though his heart
strains against the pressure; still he refuses:
There's no need. You're fussing.
I'm fine.

She drives herself to the hospital,
to the day-ward, for tests; asks a friend
to call to see him in the early afternoon;
to pretend she had not asked.

ii
By nightfall everything has changed.
His adult children, travelled home,
sit around the kitchen table,
take it in turns to break the news:
her cancer, treatable when they kissed
goodbye on the doorstep, is not treatable.

He does not look away from the truth:
she will die before him;
he will lose his wife of fifty-five years;
his carer; his home.
Someone puts a cup of tea in his hand.

iii
She comes home after seven nights –
the longest they have slept apart –
a changed woman, sunny as a schoolgirl,
high on a cocktail of drugs and denial.
She will not talk about it.
He does not know how to begin.

Her list of medicines grows longer,
her needs more complicated.
His household swarms with doctors,
nurses, carers, his adult children
back in their bedrooms,
grown knowledgeable,
opinionated.

iv
He is grateful they are there,
that she can be at home,
that he can be at home.

He wishes they would all
fuck off,
leave him in peace with her.

A storm that blows all maps away

Raiméis
for Breda Corish

You sing to me over the phone:
My Bonnie lies over the ocean,
My Bonnie lies over the sea.
I sing with you, matching your new, small voice:

Oh bring back my Bonnie to me.
It's easier on the phone. When I'm with you
I have to face the little girl who, in the space
of a week, has taken over my mother.

I'm learning to listen to your rambling stories,
to make all the little sounds -
uh-huh - yes - uh-huh - that's right -
that say I'm here, I'm listening.

I'm learning to follow your raiméis
the way I would follow a dream: *On my way into Mass last Sunday I saw the four Celtic crosses where the parish priests are buried, and at the foot of one of the crosses I saw his photo, that man, we knew him twenty years ago, Dad and myself, we used to have him out to the house for dinner. And then that man, that amadán tried to best him. You remember? You do. By God didn't he meet his match? He loved his bacon and cabbage.*

Which amadán? Who bested whom?
I'm lost. Your story winds on
like the low reaches of a slow river.
Uh-huh, I say, and *yes, yes, uh-huh.*

Breda interrupts you, takes the phone
to ask me something essential
about your opiate-sluggish bowels,
about changing a dose, a frequency.

You insist on having the phone back:
And when I came out of Mass I saw
his picture again, at the foot of his gravestone,
and he had the most beautiful smile on his face.

You put the phone down,
satisfied. You've told me what matters:
you know you're dying;
you're not afraid.

Hitting the Rapids
for Tom Sigafoos

Not the boat of you and me, love.
For now we are at lake-rest,
Lough Melvin in the evening,
watching the same two swans.

>The boat
>of my family
>has hit the rapids -
>it hurtles
>through whirlpools -
>slips in circles -
>gathers speed -
>white-water races -
>rushes -
>rocks lie hard ahead -
>no rest -
>until the final narrow cataract
>when all will disappear -
>boat, river, mother -
>into the salt-dissolving sea.

We rest from rowing, trail our hands
over the side in water so pure there are trout
found nowhere else, Sonaghan,
and Gillaroo, butter-yellow, flecked with fire.

Side-effects may occur, including euphoria
i.m. Evelyn Houlihan

Inside your breath and bone
cells multiply. You smile
fit to burst, this laughing woman
just like you on a party night.
I dance with you as you boogie
to the jazz on the radio,
your hips looser now,
more flirty than I've ever seen.

We gather round the piano
while you play: *Oh Susannah,*
now don't you cry for me.
Your fingers fly because, you tell us,
you're wearing Evelyn's ring.
We know it's the opiates
in your blood, the steroids,
maybe a secondary in your brain.

You twirl about on the piano stool:
Michael, can you find 'My Wild Irish Rose'?
He lays down the oxygen mask,
searches through scattered sheet-music,
hands you the score, manages a smile.
As soon as you turn back to the keys
he's lost.

Show Time with Teresa

The doorbell rings, the show begins.
My mother climbs her ladder,
her leotard sparkles. Her friends watch
as she twirls; as she leaps
from her platform with a story; catches
the rope-swing of their attention; pirouettes;
somersaults; throws herself at them, arms outstretched.
They catch her punch-line, laugh with her.

Her performance goes on and on.
Their faces freeze in broken smiles.
My father leaves the room.
I can't bear to listen, he whispers,
staring at the kitchen table, pushing crumbs.
*Maybe it's wrong of me. I cannot bear it
when she goes on this way.* Her laughter gales
from the sitting room: *It was
so funny. It was just
so funny.*

Teresa is not the light-hearted girl
on the high trapeze. She is the lion-tamer,
enforcing her will: No one in this house
will speak of death.

Thunder, No Rain

Heat cracks the sky...
        Suzanne Sigafoos, *Fever Season*

In Sierra Leone,
every evening at four, heat cracks the sky;
the heavens open; rain plummets down
out of charcoal-grey clouds for six solid hours.
By bedtime the air is drained of humidity.
Sleep is, briefly, possible.

Last night
sleep was not possible. All she wanted,
after I gave her a Xanax in a teaspoon of yoghurt,
was for me to look her in the eye.

Since I left childhood
(since she left childhood?)
my mother (afraid to be seen?)
looked no-one in the eye.

Last night
my mother held my gaze, her eyes hazel-green,
for a full three minutes. Then sighed,
curled on her side, slept like a child.

I lay awake,
my heart thundering a confusion
of grief, bewilderment, gratitude,
eyes wide to the night. Needing rain.

A Dying Language

New words have entered your vocabulary:
catheter; commode; zimmer-frame; suppository.
New to this house and bedroom, long acquainted

with the night-whirr of his oxygen concentrator.
Darker words, the vocabulary of the interior:
vena cava; impacted; oedema.

My sister and I are nurses again,
we read the signs of each new broken function.
We know our anatomy: the primary taking over

your core, pushing against bronchus,
aorta, oesophagus, pericardium;
your colon grown lazy from painkillers;

the feeling of skeletal cold in a leg that is warm;
that has its root in a myeloma
pressing on a tangled spinal nerve.

We know this is neuropathic pain,
the most intractable kind; that secondaries
are sprouting like seeds in your brain -

a hothouse of weeds - hot flushes back again -
your imbalanced thermo-regulatory mechanism -
your imbalanced gait - the childhood lullabies

you are singing - the miracle-tales you are telling.
Frontal lobe metastases, strange random fruit,
have altered your mind like a knife.

A gentler word: Hospice. An admission
of our failure. We thought we could do it,
my sister and I, give you the gift of a home death.

But too much is breaking down, too fast
and all together. It's hard for you to swallow now.
Hard to piss. Hard to shit. Hard to think. Hard to breathe.

Bargaining

I pray to a God I no longer believe in,
of miracle and intervention:
Please don't let her die.
I like her now.
She's been part of my life forever,
since the day I came rushing
out of her womb in a flood of blood
that nearly killed us both.

I have nothing to bargain with, God.
Only my presence.

Planets to Her Dying Sun
for Mary Corish Foley

She became our centre of gravity again,
our mother, our only child; you became
my other half through that shocked Spring,
pollen-heavy Summer, fading Autumn.
The other nurse in the family, we rarely met:
you left Saturday, I arrived Sunday;
Breda and Michael bridged the gap.

Our lovers hardly knew us: our bodies
lay between the sheets, minds half-gone
into the land of the dead. We massaged
her feet with oils, listened for the changes
in her breath, explored her skin, inch by inch,
for pressure sores. With each passing week
our love cries sounded more like grief.

When her illness outstripped the skill
of our siblings, we overlapped:
you arrived Saturday, I left Sunday.
We circled close, planets to her dying sun.
Our time at home grew shorter. Our lovers loved us,
held us when we wept. We could not, no matter
how we wished, give them the gift of sex.

October came. All the poppies gone
to seed heads, the double-flounced lilac and wine
of her garden, the pink and the crimson,
the single-skirted scarlets of the road.

On the Day of the Dead
our lives untwined.

Time on the Ocean

It has begun to seem as if this will go on forever.
               Theo Dorgan, *Time on the Ocean*

I fall asleep reading:
in the stretch of grey Atlantic
between Cape Horn and Cape Town -
four thousand nautical miles,
give or take a dip in the wave, a rise,
a storm that blows all maps away,
an out of season Westerly -
there are only two landings, *Las Malvinas*,
disputed, and *Tristan de Cunha*,
where a sailor can disembark,
two feet down on steady land.
Otherwise, it's all roll, pitch, yaw,
monotonous change.

Two months, they said,
that day she left the hospital.
We turned our lives about
so she could die at home.
Now they say she might live for a year,
because of our steadfast care.
Her heart has always been strong;
her lungs have recovered, temporarily;
only her brain is deteriorating,
the cancer changing mind and mood,
corroding memory.

I wake as light dawns,
understand: to endure the crossing
the seafarer must hold steady
in the rolling moment;
must not waste the voyage
yearning for landfall,
for Cape Town.

Homing
for Tom Sigafoos

I am weary as mud.
Cirrus clouds splay out,
frayed feathers,
move with the train.
Light slants through cumulus trees.
It's mid-July.
I've lost the date.

Like homing salmon
the train travels north-west
against the flow of the Shannon.
We pass a cabin cruiser,
a crumbled-down signal box,
a flock of birds stitching the air,
and one swift, hunting.

Sligeach, the voice says,
in his West-inflected,
curve-tongued Irish,
telling his beads
over and over:
Mainistir na Búille,
Baile an Mhóta,
Cúl Mhuine,
agus Sligeach.

My neighbour texts me.
She's seen Tom leaving
to collect me from the train.
I'm nearly home.
Sligeach.
Sligeach.
Sligeach.

The battles we fight when we can't win the war

She got you up and dressed.
I hate that orange sweater.

Doesn't suit you.
Anyway, it's far too hot.

I offer you the polka-dot summer dress,
the green cotton cardigan.

You agree to both, today
a truce in your war with death.

I leave for a break,
to read, write, walk by the river.

I return to the house. She has you again
in the orange sweater.

Rough

I'm angry with you today.
I want you to hurry up.

I'm looking for some fancy way
to say this, some honeyed metaphor.

I don't want to say it like this:
rough-cut, dumped-down.

Concrete blocks. Hard. Grey.
Abrasive.

I want you to die.

Agitation, in Three Movements

i
Two in the morning.
He shakes me awake:
She wants you and she won't tell me why.
I go in to their bedroom,
to her side of the bed: *What's wrong?*
All she can say is: *The small bag,* over and over,
pointing at the Y junction of the catheter,
then at my eye, pressing hard on the flesh
of my right temple, then at her own left eye.

I check the catheter. It's fine.
Mam, can you tell me what's bothering you?
She points at the catheter, my eye, her eye.
In the morning she will be garrulous,
almost coherent, but talk is useless now.
She holds my gaze, asking the same wordless question.
I answer her with a held silence. For five, ten, fifteen minutes:
There is no need to be afraid.

She sighs, settles to sleep.
He snores lightly beside her.

ii
I come back after my week away,
ask: *Is she still waking agitated?*
He barks at me: *Don't be ridiculous.*
How can you wake agitated? If you're asleep you're not agitated.
I'm stunned by this old version of my father.
Your mother never gets anxious.
Don't talk tripe.

No, Dad. Agitated means disturbed, restless.
I look it up in the dictionary, show him:
See?
I search for sanity more than sense -
my mother is dying, I feel like I'm losing my father.

After ten years of learned ease
I'm the awkward daughter again,
all our camaraderie gone. I must remember
what I'd schooled myself to forget:
stay downwind of the old rhinoceros
as he charges, blind, under the wound of her dying.

He storms, huffs, finally settles:
Well, he says, *if you'd been clear in the first place.*
If you'd asked me that in the first place.

iii
I have to get out of this house,
away from her need, his wound, my care.

The Gortnagearagh river flows
down from the Silvermines. I walk
between head-high mounds
of Bramble and Nettle,
gather Meadowsweet, Angelica,
bright yellow Marsh Lilies
(not Foxglove - I fear its toxic healing
in a house of broken hearts),
Rosebay Willowherb,
Wild Parsley.

Green grows into me.
My brain fills with leafy calm.
For five, ten, fifteen minutes.

Recompense

I bring you breakfast -
measure your morphine -
wait for you to choose an outfit -
get you dressed -
encourage you to drink -
do your ten o'clock meds -
walk you round the garden -
fidget while you deadhead roses -
drive to the village -
shop -
cook your dinner -
empty your catheter bag -
phone your doctor -
encourage you to drink -
measure your morphine -
you catch my hand to slow me down -

My life, you say,
would have been so much poorer without you.

A Dream of Dark Wings
after Death and the Gravedigger, *by Carlos Schwabe*

My head pounds. All week I've fretted,
wanted to be elsewhere,
impatient at my slow life while she dies.

I dream: I am making dark wings
with my father, children's wings, fashioned
of heart-shaped wire and black felt. Not pure black:

charcoal scrubbed over burnt-umber pastel.
At first we make them together,
then I post them to him, into a letterbox, as a gift.

The dream reminds me, in a homespun way,
of Schwabe's ecstatic vision:
Death crouches by an open grave,

gorgeous, fierce, compassionate. Her scythe-like wings
dip down to cradle the gravedigger:
ancient, frayed, already inside his grave.

The dream sets me wondering:
Who will die first? It could be my worn-out father,
who keeps vigil over my dying mother

as we go and come and go. It could, I suppose,
be me. The dream is mine. My impatience
at the slowness of her death might die.

Whoever it is, however it is:
my hammering week-long headache is gone.

Dust
for Esther O'Brien

We disagree: who cares for her, and how, who pays,
who sides with whom, who loves her more, and him.
After the fight that every family falls through
when sibling-strangers are flung together to attend
a slowly dying mother - after the angry e-mails
and the bitter phone calls - after the shock of learning
how far apart we are, how deeply we disagree -
Martha, Magdalen, Thomas, Peter -
even Pilate, even Judas - how different we are,
the gods that we honour - after all the dust has settled
and we're back in the river, pulling together, oar-stroke
by oar-stroke, no coxswain to guide us, sculling in time -
after the fierce, brief battle of our worst, wounded selves -
nothing has changed. She is dying.

Wild Love

When I am an old woman I shall...
pick flowers in other people's gardens.
                    Jenny Joseph, *Warning*

The mother I grew up with prayed every night
that her sexual, godless children
would return to the straight and narrow drill
where she'd planted and baptised them
like cabbages, half a rough century ago.

In her final months my mother spoke of God
as He-She-It, as the boundaries
in her brain disintegrated, as the cancer
scattered seeds of grief and dread, occasional joy.

My mother's God of rules had no dominion over nature.
She picked flowers from other people's gardens
long before she grew old.
Stole cuttings, imported forbidden roots,
'acquired' seed-heads.

If she thought she could get away with it,
if she wanted something badly enough
to increase and multiply the fecundity of her garden,
the wanton riot of her half-wild beds.

In her final months my mother loved us all -
willowy grandchildren, bolted offspring, tangled sister -
with the same wild love she had once reserved
for her crimson-poppy, moon-white-daisy,
tiger-lily garden.

The dead are gathering to gather you in

Stripped of Everything

It's hard not knowing how it will end.
That was the first time,
in four months, you acknowledged
it might not end well.
And you've taken to reminiscing
about the summer when your brother died
as if you were comparing like
with like.

Even so.
I am going to peel myself away
from this constant care.
I've donned the iron bra
to stop my milk from flowing.
I want, for just three weeks,
to not be milk-tugged by your open mouth.

Only what you wanted yesterday
was not milk. You wanted the truth,
however bitter. *No hugs*, you cried.
For God's sake give me some privacy,
am I to be stripped of everything?

I stood by your bedroom door:
I'll leave you be then?
No, no, you said. *Stay.*
I just need to rant.
The dam had to break sometime.

You raised your eyes to mine:
And is there, you asked,
pointing at the centre of your chest,
really a problem?

There is, I said.
Yes.

Mater

Touch.
Not a lover's.
A woman who doesn't talk
lays oiled hands on my back
and I know *Mother*,
though you're dying,
I know *Home*.

For one hour
I don't talk,
don't think.
Am body.
Am breath.
Am child.
Am.

Seven Winters
for Trish Howley

Once I lived beneath a lemon tree,
wore sandals all year long,

air on my skin, mud squelching
between my toes after sudden rain.

Seven winters have passed
since I last saw Africa, and I miss her:

a large and exuberant friend
who wears colours that clash,

who laughs louder than anyone else
in the restaurant, who sucks lustily on crab claws,

on the sour bite of a lemon.
I want to live with her again,

I want to make my house in a corner
of her courtyard, to smell like her,

of sandalwood, to watch her enormous
and flexible hips as she dances.

I want to live for one season more in a land
where rain is always a blessing.

O Summer, O Africa, O Deathless Mama,
make a place for me at your table.

Respite

I sleep
and in my dreaming
sleep again

Give me the Death I Need
… dadme la muerte que me falta…
                        Rosario Castellanos

I want to be able to hold death
tenderly, like a baby.
To say it's only death, old friend,
old trouble. To look steady
into that circle of night,
your grave.

the aurora borealis is inside your head,
your shattered eye is glowing,
your eyes, one adult, one child,
are giving birth to fire

I'm standing, fierce,
outside the gate of heaven,
a rebel in your garden,
your empty-handed
open-hearted daughter
watching poppies flare and die.

you are doing the job you came to do,
pushing through the fracture zone,
talking to maybe-angels,
racing to the finish

Whose eyes are open,
yours or mine? I need,
not knowing if it's life or death,
to get the balance right:
to hold you like a mother;
to look you in the burning eye.

The House of the Double-Headed Axe

It's like the summer Pat died, isn't it?
It is, I say, emptying your catheter bag.
But no one's dying this summer, are they?

Your question is a labrys. You press a blade
Against my heart, demand hope; twist the axe about;
Press a blade against my throat, demand truth.

In the house of the double-headed axe, I freeze.
Between the blades of truth and lie I find no answer.
You understand my silence perfectly,

Retreat from me in fury.
For seven ice-fire days and nights
You sever your link with my twice-broken heart.

Six weeks later you are dead.
Nine months before I understand.
I gave you what you needed:

A scarlet thread to navigate the labyrinth
Between denial and acceptance;
A single sword to slay your fearful minotaur;

A way to be angry.

Rage

*I am tired of all these nurses
and their different systems.
I am not a child.
Do not treat me like a child.*

You go to bed angry, tearful.
Wake the same,
fiercely independent,
barely able to move.
You struggle upright, perch
on the edge of the bed,
pull on your trousers.
You lurch down the hallway,
your trousers at half-mast,
loose about your heels,
half-unzipped.
I'm terrified you'll stumble.
I know what your hipbone
looks like, X-rayed:
a delicate tracery
of cancerous metastases;
calcified lace.
If you fall,
your life at home
is over: ambulance,
accident and emergency,
a hospital death.

You refuse my arm:
*Thank you very much,
I am perfectly stable.*

Bitter Honey

I hand you your tablets,
you hand me a request, written
in your newly-wavering hand:
*Please play One Day at a Time
over and over on a loop.
Sometimes He needs some help
so He can help us.*

Sweet Jesus, not an hour
of Country and Western piety!
But when I set it playing -
I'm only human, I'm just a woman...
the rhythm's too good to resist,
my hips start swaying
the way you love to see
and you laugh.

The air in this house
is shadowed with sorrow and golden,
like honey gleaned
from bitter herbs.

Back Where We Started

He holds your hand while I invent
a makeshift sterile trolley.
With his other hand
he tunes the dial to Sunday Mass,
broadcast from the church in the village.
He's cracking jokes: *I bet you never thought
you'd be listening to Mass like this!*

As Father Ryan welcomes the congregation
into the church and onto the radio
I open the Foley catheter (14 French, 10 ml),
put on a pair of sterile gloves (Latex-free, size 7),
half-laugh: *I haven't been this intimate
with you since the day I was born.*
You smile at me,
nervous but trusting.

I haven't catheterised anyone in eighteen years,
since I last worked on a ward.
While the choir sings the *Kyrie*
I remove the gloves,
go to my bedroom,
power up the laptop, Google,
find an image, remind myself
of the exact anatomy.

I open another pair of gloves,
search for the spot.
You are steroid-swollen down there,
but my aim is true: urine flows.
Alleluia, we're home and dry,
no need for nappies today.
I connect the catheter bag. Father Ryan
proclaims the gospel on the radio.

Daughter Number Two

Today,
you could not remember my name.
Later you wrote it down, circled it,
kept it before you all day long,
an *aide memoire*.

Today,
for the first time, I understood.
The woman I am when I am with you
will die when you die:
second-born; swift-born; blood-born;
daughter who, too often, says,
Don't, you'll hurt yourself,
who dances with you to the old 78s;
who looks you in the eye when you're afraid.

Today,
it's only my name you've forgotten.
You're not gone yet.
I am still Daughter-Stay-Safe,
Daughter-Shimmy, Daughter-Honest-Eye.

Daughter-Number-Two.

The Skill of Lipstick

You gave up on the bra last week:
Too awkward. Too uncomfortable.
Still insist on the make-up:
Lipstick, at the very least.

Upper lip - two swoops - a dip in the middle.
Lower lip - one swoop - press the lips together.
The movements practiced, unforgettable,
like twirling a Quickstep.

The piano defeated you today.
For two hours you sat, frozen,
Dad's hand on the small of your back:
I can't get started.

You couldn't remember how to move your
fingers. It wasn't that you were trying to
recollect a tune. You were trying to
remember, in your fingers, the
lift and
fall, lift and
fall, how to
connect, how to
touch
fingertip to
ivory -

You will lose
your skill with lipstick.

Wing Mirror, Butterfly
for Nancy McNamara

In the first silence of this frantic day
I hear the rattle in your lungs, grown louder,
stronger. I know you could die like this,

drowning. I know I can manage
your distress with morphine.
But Dad? My aunt? My brother,

on the road from Dublin? My sisters,
flying in from London?
I don't want them to hear you die like this.

I ring the Hospice, beg the night nurse:
I have ampoules of Buscopan in the house
to dry her up, but no needles or syringes.

Can you give me needles and syringes?
I clip a wing mirror driving through the village.
She talks me through doses, frequency,

how to insert a sub-cutaneous butterfly.
I drive home, pierce your skin with the tiny needle,
inject. Wait an hour.

Your breath becomes, briefly, a little less wet,
less loud; a little less
like drowning.

The Doorway into the Invisible

The roses in your garden *whisper, whisper.*
The woman you were grows smaller.
It's night-time now, good night.
Thank you so much, you say.
I'm so glad I can be at home.
And can I leave the radio on?
It's bedtime now, little mother,
I'll sing you a song: *Seóthín, seóthó,
mo stóirín, mo leanbh,* the song you sing
when you're frightened,
this is how we know, *whisper,
whisper...*

You do not ask out loud, not once,
until you're ready to know without doubt,
and then no need to whisper:
I'll be leaving soon, you say,
I'll be going to America,
to be with Pat and Evelyn.
Your dead brother, your dead sister.
There is no need to *whisper,
whisper...*

You like the doorway into the invisible
that has opened up on your left,
the unpainted rectangle of wall by your bed,
old pink against new green,
hidden for years by the wardrobe,
too big to move when you painted the room,
until we had to tug and haul, make space
for your hospital bed. I'll be leaving soon,
you say, there is no need to *whisper,
whisper...*

In your garden roses fall,
even the fierce yellow rose.
The year has turned, it is *Samhain,*
the dead are hovering,
we are still singing,
you have only breath to *whisper...*

The living arrive, your son, you smile,
but time is unravelling,
the dead are gathering
to gather you in, breath
is hard labour.

Your daughters arrive,
your eldest, your youngest.
Your eyes can flicker,
only flicker. Roses
whisper

*

whisper rest.
Your husband begins the Rosary,
the Glorious Mystery,
Glory be to the Father and to the Son.
We murmur the half-remembered,
never-forgotten answers.

Our Mother who art in heaven,
hallowed be thy name,
and thy still breath and thy bloated body,
and all the medicines on the windowsill,
and the tiny needle under thy skin
that gave thee ease in the end times,
Amen.

Then the house of the living must sleep
before the long hard day ahead.
But first a lullaby, the cradle song
you sang to us, we touch to gather strength,
we sing to you: *Toora Loora Loora,*
hush now don't you cry.

Hush now, whisper.
Roses whisper.
Good now.
Whisper.
Night.

Between *Samhain* and All the Saints

Sunday evening, six o'clock, October 30th.
Time for your new, stronger antibiotic.
You begin to groan:
Oh feck. Oh feck. Oh feck.
Sin a bhfuil.
Oh feck. Oh feck. Oh let me go. Oh feck.
Sin a bhfuil.
I don't let him near you till the morphine kicks in,
but he hears enough.

And again at two in the morning,
when I wake you for your Paracetamol.
Oh feck, you cry from your hospital bed,
beside his single bed. *Oh feck*.
As I leave the room he whispers:
I think I'm going to let her go.
I kiss him on the forehead:
We'll talk about it in the morning.

I lie in bed, fretting: this isn't just an infection.
Pleural effusion? Pressure on your Vena Cava?
I curse the bank holiday weekend -
I need your own GP to visit,
or your Hospice Home Care nurse -
that on-call doctor was worse than useless,
a plumber making a house call. Cerebral oedema?

Helpless to help you, he wakes me at seven:
Mam's in distress again.
I give you morphine, a drink, get you settled.
He and I sit down together over breakfast.
He says it again: *I think I'm going to let her go.*
My heart is racing. *I'm with you, Dad.*
Even if she recovers, she'll go this way in the end.
We stop all the antibiotics.

You die very quietly.
One thirty in the morning.
Tuesday, November 1st.
The Feast of All Saints.

The Wake

Friends come and go all day.
Rosaries are said. Tea made.
Chat about the weather.
Nothing special. One last chance
to sit with you, in the absence
of your presence.

There is a quiet hour
in the late morning.
I lie on his bed, head to toe
with you in your hospital bed.
Beneath the gold satin eiderdown
my right palm rests on your still-warm shin.

I see you breathe.
The body is a creature of habit.
My eyes cannot stop seeing,
certain as my own breath, your breath.

I force my eyes to notice the shine
on the quilted satin, the way it does not move,
the pattern of bright gold and dull gold
over your chest, your breasts.
The way it does not alter.

I lie beside you for an hour. Each time
I think I see you breathe, I force my eyes
to relinquish their illusion, accept the still truth,
until the cord of my faith in your breath,
unquestioned since the hour
I formed in your womb,

is severed.

Final Intimacies
for Maureen Cox

Silk underwear
Because you loved the feel
The warmth of silk on your skin
Your pink pashmina
Your best brooch
A circlet of gold and pearls
Your brown-and-white polka dot dress
Your chocolate-coloured turtleneck
Pink bed socks to match your pashmina
Your sister's mother-of-pearl rosary beads.

We hand our choices
Into the hands of the undertaker
For the final intimacies.

Next day we gather early
Try out your pearls
Choose the gold clip-on earrings
Adjust your makeup
Curl your hair.

Before he opens
The funeral parlour doors
To admit the waiting village
We sing our cradle song
One more time:

Hush now don't you cry.

Tears still come, a salt surprise

Filling the Skip
for Mike Corish

We make a clearance of the house,
break up what's left of the furniture,
fit it neatly into the second skip.

All your treasures - your *tricky-tracks*
and *purdies* - will go to the charity shop.
Your lexicon will die with us.

We save love letters, photographs,
receipts from your honeymoon.

Breda gathers viburnum, narcissi,
pale yellow broom: final gifts
for your daughter-in-law, your sister, your grave.

Mike saves a single leg
from the table where we ate as children.

Mary makes a shrine in your bedroom:
a vase of daffodils, six tea-lights.
One each: her, him, the four of us.

I hold back a single mattress from the skip,
in case Mike needs to make a final visit;
bedding for one; a towel; a kettle; a saucepan;

six cups, six spoons, six plates,
six knives, six forks.
I close the door.

Advice from My Dead Mother

She has the thighs and breasts of a Goddess,
and the petalled eye of a Buddha.
Yes, she says, *it's true. The sun is my son.*
Casual as you please.

My father roars, his lungs snared in breath,
his flesh trapped in the teeth of life.
She is unshaken. She moves
the way a tree moves, waves a greeting.

*For as long as he cannot cup
my death in his palms,* she says
as she weaves the rainbow,
his song can only be loud, be broken.

*But even the moving sun will come to rest
beyond the horizon, and wake refreshed.*

Fetish, Reprise

I dream I've lost her button box,
it's like losing her again.
Things hold her to me:
her woolen winter coat;
her mother's sapphire engagement ring;
her heavy silver bracelet;
her walnut button box,
inlaid and burled, varnished and battered.

My mother was a pagan.
I touch the things she loved,
I know myself loved still.

Lady Rain
for Mary Corish Foley

After my sister's wedding –
intimate; sacramental;
as happy as her fascinator,
red roses in her hair;
as her smile of shy surprise
when we all applauded
after '*husband and wife*' –
after our burst of rowdy *craic*
in the pale of chapel and vestment –
after a no-drama kind of day,
except for the light
spilling out of the clouds
like silver lady-rain –

Grief strikes like a kestrel,
without reason –
her talons
at my throat,
her hooked beak
plucking
at my eyes,
her predator wings
calling blood
to my blood –

My silver-grey mother, absent
from your first-born daughter's wedding.

The Butcher, The Lacemaker

God is tenderising me today.
A spiked wooden mallet slams

into a piece of steak
over and over

and over again. It works,
this treatment. It's effective.

It breaks the fibres. The steak
begins to look like lace.

Once I give in
I don't mind so much.

I begin to enjoy the feeling
of being pummelled, loosened,

and then the flick of the fine lace hook
in God's dextrous fingers,

putting me together again,
tenderly, to a new design.

My Father Faced Death in Full Knowledge

Two days before he died - though his death
seemed weeks away to me, or months -
he phoned his bank; took a breath of oxygen
between each sentence; gave instructions
for a transfer of funds;
paid for his funeral.

My father, constant warrior, met death
without a fight: the day before he died,
his oxygen machine stopped working.
Under his direction I disentangled a nest
of tubes and connections; re-routed the line
from the back-up machine; extended the tubing
into the bathroom; tested the system
for leaks. Not one sharp word throughout,
despite my worried fumblings.
As if he had been, all his life,
a man of peace.

My father asked death to wait awhile.
The morning of the day he died he said:
It's time to call them home.
Throughout the morning he asked for updates
on their flights. His fingertips and earlobes grey,
breath short, skin clammy.
I wrapped crushed ice in baby-wipes,
stroked his forehead and temples;
his neck; his wrists and hands.
His daughters and son-in-law arrived.
He greeted them by name: *Mary; Breda; Colin.*
I gave them fresh ice for the baby-wipes.
That's nice, he said. And then, gently,
That's enough for now.
Thanks.

My father slept alone for twenty months
and twenty-four declining nights.
We laid him down beside her: Michael on the right,
Teresa on the left, as in their marriage bed.

Imbolc
for Cys Corish

Three Celtic crosses tilt
against a mackerel sky:

> Perpendicular beams tempered by a mandala,
> host in the monstrance, circle of wholeness;
> no broken body here, no dead wood -
> lichen lives and spreads on hand-cut,
> wind-chiselled stone.

Death might be like this,
company, not Calvary:

> Gossiping crosses huddle, share the latest news;
> a whole family sprawls through a graveyard,
> their new home a church of stone
> held together by holly, ivy, mistletoe;
> fire-berries blaze in the hearth.

Growing old
might be like this:

> The people you have loved exchange amiable gossip
> on the sunrise side of a stone wall.
> You cannot hear what they say;
> on your side of the wall it is quiet.
> Quieter by the year.

Caprice
After I and the Village, *by Marc Chagall*

Only connect! said E. M. Forster,
but my goat said it first. Also:
Look me in the eye. Touch my hide.
Milk me in the morning, the way your mother did.
Paint your house bright yellow.
Touch the tree of life.

Only connect.
You'll lose that green, unhealthy look
from too much time inside;
you'll find the iris of your eye;
you'll recollect the night.

Only connect.
Don't forget.
Don't play the violin
while standing on your head.
Don't fall in love
with Mister Death.

The Old World Slips Away

i
6:20 on a January morning,
the plane tilts south over Dublin.
The old lady, pretty as I've ever seen,

wears every jewel she owns -
diamond-bright head lights,
sodium-lamp sparklers, ruby-red tail lights.

Silk-scarf dawn over the island of Madeira,
a river of sky in a continent of cloud,
cliffs whiter than Dover.

Mt Teide rises
from her downy no-tog duvet
neat as the nipple of a young one.

Descent, through archipelagos of cloudlets,
slo-mo airy snails,
feather boas.

On the ferry we follow Columbus,
dozing through safety messages whistled in *Silbo*.
The old world slips away.

ii
From San Sebastien de la Gomera
the blue bus twines up the mountain
into the Greenwood.

Misty twisted thickets
of laurel and cedar, the charcoal ghosts
of trees from fires last May -

unlike this old volcano, lightning
never sleeps. I close my eyes,
wake to blindness,

tunnel darkness.
Then we're pinning down
the hairs of the road, so steep it

curls back on itself,
three sides round a wayside church:
terracotta tiles, dust-dulled tangerine.

We check into the apartment,
find a harbour restaurant,
order *paella*,

wait. You drink a *cerveza*.
I walk the margin of the sea,
her white rim sharp against dark volcanic sand.

Awake in the night I hear her
tossing the hem of her beaded skirt,
urged on by the round of the white-gold moon:

taffeta - taffeta - taffeta -
lace - lace - lace -
taffeta - taffeta - taffeta -
lace - lace -
taffeta - taffeta -
lace -

Grief, Uncomplicated

Grief is a frayed sweater I wear on remembrance days,
when tears come, a salt surprise.

Most days I dress up spruce, your proud daughter,
doing fine. Each year digs you deeper,

Limerick clay moulding close to your bones,
knitting into the thread of your polka dot dress,

into the velveteen weft of the kitten you hugged,
snug in a corner of your coffin, for comfort.

We did well, mother of mine: I grew to love you
straight, without tangles of need;

you loved me honest, the way I always wanted.
Dying, you looked me in the eye.

Dreamtime

I dream only words,
a disembodied voice:

Remember when you were a giraffe
on the plains of Africa
with your mother
and you were two years old.

No sense to that sentence, not even in dreamtime,
only the sense of truth and absolute love:

the wide plains around Nairobi, stretching south
to Masai Mara, the Serengeti, and beyond;

my mother and I, she tall as the tops of acacias,
me solid on long legs, still staying close;

and out of the ground and the air around us
and the warm round sun, love.

Glossary

Suud: The great swamp in South Sudan through which the White Nile flows, home to the Dinka, Nuer and Shilluk peoples.

Raiméis: Nonsense.

Amadán: Fool.

Seóthín, seóthó, mo stóirín, mo leanbh: Shush, hush, my treasure, my child.

Sin a bhfuil: That's it, that's all.

Silbo: The whistled language of the island of La Gomera in the Canary Islands, used to communicate across deep ravines.

About the author

Monica Corish earned a degree in science and an MA in Development Studies, and she trained as a nurse. She worked in Africa for many years as a primary health care adviser with Irish and international NGOs, and she wrote a manual on healthcare in refugee and conflict settings for the World Health Organisation. In 2005 a cervical disc injury brought an end to her nursing and overseas development careers. In the same year she moved to Co Leitrim, where she now lives.

She was awarded an Arts Council Literature Bursary in 2009, and was shortlisted for the Patrick Kavanagh Poetry Award in 2010. *Slow Mysteries*, her first poetry collection, was published by Doghouse Books in 2012. In 2014-15 she was chosen as SPARK writer-in-residence at the Leitrim Observer; her collection/anthology *Gleanings - Poetry Inspired by the Leitrim Observer* was published by Leitrim Arts Office in 2015. She received bursaries from Arts and Disability Awards Ireland and Leitrim Arts Office to develop *A Dying Language*, inspired mainly by the experience of nursing her mother when she was dying of cancer.

Monica serves as editor of the monthly Writing Leitrim Page in the Leitrim Observer, and as a judge for the Allingham Festival Poetry and Flash Fiction competitions. She leads writing workshops in the North West and in Dublin: see www.monicacorish.ie.

www.ingramcontent.com/pod-product-compliance
Lightning Source LLC
LaVergne TN
LVHW021717080426
835510LV00010B/1005